L. IS FOR SAYERS
A Play in Five Acts

by

Victoria Nelson

DREAMING SPIRES **PUBLICATIONS**

Updated First Edition 2013
Copyright © 2009 Victoria Nelson
All rights reserved.

ISBN: 061553872X
ISBN-13: 9780615538723
Registration #PAu3-423-086

ACKNOWLEDGEMENTS

My heartfelt acknowledgement goes to the members of my family and friends whose continual inspiration, well deserved admonitions and unwavering confidence in me made this work possible. I am especially grateful to my mom who supported me endlessly with her ideas, prayers, and valuable criticisms, and who through longsuffering endured my ceaseless orating and floor pacing as I struggled to complete this project over the last 12 years. I am also indebted to Joseph Pearce who encouraged me with his enthusiasm and generous gift of time. Of all those who have given me their support over the years, I am truly thankful to Reverend John McGregor, SM and Velma B. Richmond, PhD who took a little hippie girl and guided her feet towards a wiser path and who never lost faith in her ability to keep always in sight of that path.

A SPECIAL THANK YOU

This updated edition of <u>L. is for Sayers: A Play in Five Acts</u> was made possible through the kind assistance, patience, and untiring effort of Jasmine Simeone, Secretary and Bulletin Editor for the Dorothy L. Sayers Society in England. My deepest appreciation goes to Jasmine for helping me to ensure that the work is an honest portrayal of the life and writing of Dorothy L. Sayers as well as a historically accurate representation of the period in which she lived. From the outset, the chief purpose of the work has been to capture Sayers' worldview and reflect her values. It is hoped that this updated edition will continue to inspire readers to learn more about Sayers and her outstanding contribution to the literary arts.

INTRODUCTION

By almost any measurement, Dorothy Leigh Sayers was one of the giants of the first half of the twentieth century. As a scholar, writer, and a public speaker, she excelled. The reluctance of her world to grant her appropriate acclaim is partly because of the very diversity and character of her accomplishments.

Nancy M. Tischler
Dorothy L. Sayers: A Pilgrim Soul

The many shades and nuances of Sayers' life and writing lend themselves well to a play. One in particular stands out—her creation of that ever cheerful, indomitable romantic hero, Lord Peter Wimsey. Who more fitted to narrate and sing praise of her varied and distinctive accomplishments? The work is essentially a celebration of Sayers' life and writing, but is also filled with good humor and flights of fancy and is intended to introduce her literary legacy to a whole new generation. Only the vehicle of drama has been added to this imaginative account to bring her work and values to light.

When Sayers said "I have a careless rage for life," she meant just that come what may. And those familiar with the Mind of the Maker may be able to observe how her love of life grew and matured until it became all-in-all for her. And it is Sayers' passion for life and for Literature that serves as both theme and plot. The narrative thread moving through L. is

<u>for Sayers</u> illustrates the growth of an individual, a thinker and writer, whose actions demonstrate the relationship between learning, experience, and desire, and the choices we sometimes make as a consequence.

We have witnessed the transformation of the Age of Information into the Age of Entertainment. Yet this prodigious development, the mark of a high civilization, comes with a price for artists and writers. As a driving force in business, healthcare, education, and art, "entertainment," especially in the form of digital graphics, now serves to sustain and advance our culture. Young people today are communicating continuously in various performance modes through chatting, role playing in virtual worlds and online video games, and sharing ideas via social networks. It also seems that there are increasing numbers of individuals interested in scriptwriting and filmmaking, yet we must be sure to supply them with what Sayers describes as the "tools of learning".

At its heart, the play is a tribute to higher education and may have a special appeal to homeschooling families and those interested in introducing young people to the Great Books. An inherent feature of the work is the way in which the various roles require readers and performers to extend themselves linguistically, culturally and intellectually. A master of characterization and of the ability to defend the dignity of the human person, Sayers was quintessentially a woman both of, and very much ahead of her time.

DRAMATIS PERSONAE
(in order of appearance)

RADIO ANNOUNCER

OXFORD STUDENTS

BICYCLIST

AGING DON

LORD PETER WIMSEY, amateur sleuth, criminologist, and man of the world

OLDER SAYERS, Dorothy L. Sayers, scholar, novelist, playwright and creator of Lord Peter Wimsey

EMILY PENROSE, principal of Somerville College

YOUNGER SAYERS, Dorothy L. Sayers

JIM, Muriel Jaeger, Sayers' close friend, Somerville classmate and member of MAS (Mutual Admiration Society)

TONY, Catherine Godfrey, Sayers' close friend, Somerville classmate and member of MAS

FEMALE STUDENTS, Somervillians

MISS POPE, Mildred Pope, Somerville don and Sayers' mentor

MISS BRUCE, Alice Bruce, Somerville don and vice principal

BILL WHITE, father of Sayers' son John Anthony

DOCTOR, Alice Chance, medical doctor, Sayers' neighbor and friend

NURSE, assistant to Alice Chance

1st FEMALE TYPIST, employee at Benson's

2nd FEMALE TYPIST, employee at Benson's

MALE COPYWRITER, employee at Benson's

MAC, Atherton Fleming, husband of Dorothy L. Sayers

BUNTER, manservant and friend of Lord Peter Wimsey

HARRIET VANE, mystery writer and well-known companion of Lord Peter Wimsey

VICTIM and MURDERER

PARKER, Chief Inspector at Scotland Yard, friend and brother-in-law of Lord Peter Wimsey

POLICEMAN

AKEDEMOS

THE POLITICIAN and POLITICIAN'S AUDIENCE

THE SCHOLAR and SCHOLAR'S AUDIENCE

THE ARTIST

THE STUDENT

THE TEACHER

BOETHIUS

THE SEVEN LIBERAL ARTS

LADY RHETORICA

LADY WISDOM and CHILDREN of LADY WISDOM

ADÈLE, unwed mother cared for by Dorothy L. Sayers

SOMERVILLE DONS and SCOUT

ACT I
Scene 1

SETTING: Oxford, England during the first half of the 20th Century.

MUSIC: Plays for a brief interval then fades (e.g. Charleston (1925) – Cecile Mack and Jimmy Johnson, Remarkable Girl (1929) – Country Washburne).

RADIO ANNOUNCER (V.O.) That was Remarkable Girl played by Ted Weems and his Orchestra. And it's a remarkable girl who serves a sandwich made with Coleman's Mustard. Coleman's English Mustard by special appointment to (His Majesty) the King. Today, the 6th of August, we celebrate the anniversary of another remarkable girl, American Athlete Gertrude Ederle, who at the age of nineteen became the first woman to swim the English Channel. Greetings and best wishes to you Miss Ederle from your neighbors across the sea. (pause) Do you have trouble falling asleep at night? Are you listless and irritable during the day? Then try Ovaltine, nature's tonic at bedtime. Safe and nutritious, drink Ovaltine at bedtime and sleep your cares away. (pause) You have been listening to Radio Luxembourg. And now Collegiana . . .

MUSIC: Instrumental piece appropriate to an academic setting (e.g. Collegiana (1928) – Jimmy McHugh and Dorothy Fields, Everything's

Gonna Be Alright (1926) – Coon Sanders) plays briefly then fades.

SOUND: Great Tom of Christ Church or multiple bells throughout Oxford University ring briefly then fade.

LIGHTING: Fade in to reveal the backdrop of an Oxford College (e.g. Christ Church) quad and walkway in foreground.

RISE: OXFORD STUDENTS dressed in period clothing, wearing long or short academic gowns, some carrying books and wearing college scarves, stroll leisurely about. A BICYCLIST, a young black-robed don with books strapped to her rear fender, pedals across the stage, ringing her bell.

SOUND: Bicycle bell, birds singing (e.g. English sparrow), and the muffled voices of students engaged in heady discussions.

RISE (CONT'D):   An AGING DON in an ill-fitted gown and mortarboard hurries past, carrying an armload of books and papers muttering to himself. LORD PETER WIMSEY emerges from the bustle of activity. He is dressed in academic robe with subfusc and monocle and strolls downstage center.

PROLOGUE

LORD PETER WIMSEY: Ah, Oxford! Ancient city, abode of scholars and simple folk. Of books and stones and wooden halls, of after-dinner walks in the Fellows' garden, evenings of blossoms and friendship. I can see the Cherwell silently winding its way past Magdalen and Christ Church Meadow. I'm a Balliol man myself, name Lord Peter Wimsey and rather well known . . . (affixes his monocle) but I digress. It's not about myself, this city or of its colleges that I have come to speak, but of its progeny – of one spawned in its waters of erudition and excellence, one who, like so many before her, has experienced the mystery and magic of Oxford. (as he concludes his soliloquy, the hubbub of Oxford fades and he motions downstage left which has been kept in the dark)

LIGHTING: Fadeout on Oxford. Spot downstage left to reveal the OLDER SAYERS sitting at her desk.

WIMSEY (CONT'D): I speak of Dorothy Leigh Sayers. (walks towards her desk)

DIRECTION: *The OLDER SAYERS is wearing her pince nez and appears to be deep in thought. The desk is littered with books and papers. She is illuminated by the glow of a period floor lamp and there are stacks of books sitting on the floor near her desk. WIMSEY is invisible to her.*

WIMSEY (CONT'D): (stands a little distance from the desk and addresses the audience) Sayers was born in Oxford

WIMSEY (CONT'D): on the 13th of June 1893. She was the delightful little orchid, cultivated and pampered, flourishing at the center of her family's household. Her father began instructing her in Latin at age 6. In a short time, she mastered French and German and could speak both languages fluently. She continued to be homeschooled until age 15. During these formative years, she mesmerized her family and friends by putting on plays and writing long narrative poetry. In 1911, at the age of eighteen, she contracted an illness that resulted in the loss of her hair. And for a time she was forced to wear a wig. From 1912-1915 she attended Somerville, an Oxford ladies' college founded in 1879. Although she excelled in her studies and was keen on her appearance, she had on occasion been criticized for her outlandish mode of dress, loud voice, and outspoken opinions. But it was here at Oxford where she made her mark and left the world an enduring legacy of remarkable wit and high-minded intellectual achievement.

DIRECTION: WIMSEY *exits center stage disappearing into the darkness.*

End Scene 1

ACT I
Scene 2

LIGHTING: Fade in to reveal an Oxford lecture hall
              (1915).

DIRECTION: *The lecturer standing behind a podium is EMILY
              PENROSE. Present are the YOUNGER SAY-
              ERS, her friends JIM and TONY, and several
              other FEMALE STUDENTS. They are sitting
              in chairs facing the speaker. Some are holding pen-
              cils and have notepads on their laps.*

EMILY PENROSE: In conclusion, I don't need to remind
you that some of you will be going down this year – 1915
marking yet another generation of distinguished graduates
from an Oxford ladies' college. However, I hear that some of
our new first-years, with the support of the thirds I might
add, are already making suggestions to disregard some of
our outmoded conventions. As your principal, I beg you to
be patient. We are poised on the edge of a precipice. From
here women's education can either take flight and soar, or
suffer an injurious setback. Nevertheless, we at Somerville
will remain firm in our aim to secure membership in the
University, thus becoming the recipient of degrees despite
our reputation in some quarters (leans forward) of being
"difficult". My fight, as you know, has always been on your
behalf and I have every confidence in your success. Good
afternoon ladies.

DIRECTION: EMILY PENROSE exits and the FEMALE STUDENTS disperse exiting right and left stage, leaving JIM, TONY, and the YOUNGER SAYERS alone in the lecture hall.

JIM: I say Dorothy, speaking of outmoded conventions don't you think you're being a bit overzealous as Bicycle Secretary? That new first year is rather upset with you. She parked her bike in front of the SCR (Senior Common Room) just long enough to deliver a note. And when she came out the bike was gone! She told me you impounded it.

TONY: Yes, she mentioned that to me as well. (to the YOUNGER SAYERS) Maybe you're in training to work for Scotland Yard.

JIM: Or perhaps brother Sayers, you will one day write a detective mystery about a notorious bicycle thief.

TONY: Oh yes. (places the right hand over her eyes and looks to the right) We seek him here, (then alternately places the left hand and looks to the left) we seek him there[1] (keeping her left hand over her eyes, she bends a little forward pretending to have spotted someone in the distance) last seen riding a tandem across the quad of a well known ladies college!

JIM: She certainly has the imagination for it don't you know.

YOUNGER SAYERS: Alright. Steady on you two. I will speak to her about it. I suppose I get carried away sometimes

---

1   From The Scarlet Pimpernel (1905) Baroness Emmuska Orczy.

YOUNGER SAYERS (CONT'D): "For Zeal's a dreadful termagant that teaches Saints to tear and rant."[2]

TONY: Quite right. Shall we go for a walk then? Dorothy, did you bring your cigarettes?

DIRECTION: *The three companions walk slowly towards the right stage exit while light-heartedly conversing with one another.*

JIM: (imitating EMILY PENROSE) Ladies, "we are poised on the edge of a precipice."

TONY: Makes one feel a little like Daedalus.[3]

JIM: No Tony, more like Dido[4] ruling her bit of land surrounded by men on every side.

YOUNGER SAYERS: I agree. But Dido was admired. We, on the other hand, are merely tolerated.

TONY: That's a very interesting point. But why should we be intimidated? After all we're here to stay. I can't see the Pen ever giving up.

JIM: And falling on her sword? (doubles over pretending to stab herself in imitation of Dido)

---

2   Samuel Butler, Hudibras (1663-1680) Part III, Canto II, Ln. 675. Enjoyed by Sayers as an adolescent.
3   Refers to the myth of Daedalus who built a set of wings for himself and his son and was able to fly away from a high tower where they were imprisoned. See Virgil, The Aeneid (29-19 BC).
4   Queen Dido used the sword of Aeneas to kill herself after he abandoned her. The Aeneid (29-19 BC).

YOUNGER SAYERS: Oh, she's far too sensible for that. You have to admire the courage of our dons. Where would we be without them?

DIRECTION: *As the three companions exit right stage, two Somerville dons in conversation enter left stage and walk towards the lecture hall.*

MISS POPE: She has a brilliant mind, our Miss Sayers.

MISS BRUCE: Yes Miss Pope, a true scholar's mind. Unfortunately not everyone will be sympathetic to her view of life.

MISS POPE: She has a scholar's mind certainly, but she is also a temperamental and good-hearted soul. I fairly believe she will suffer much disappointment during her life.

LIGHTING: Spot on the OLDER SAYERS as MISS POPE is speaking.

DIRECTION: *The OLDER SAYERS rises from her desk and moves center stage where the two professors are standing.*

MISS POPE (CONT'D): The combination of intellect and strong emotion is a difficult balancing act. It can lead one into all sorts of compromising circumstances.

OLDER SAYERS: (standing in the midst of the two professors) Had I known myself better, what could I have done to change the course of my life? Would it have been possible?

DIRECTION: *MISS POPE and MISS BRUCE continue speaking about her as in answer to her question but they are not aware of her presence because she is invisible to them.*

MISS BRUCE: Alas, it's not possible to change one's nature, not in a thousand lifetimes.

MISS POPE: Quite true Miss Bruce. I wish her all the best. But true love, marriage, a settled family life, these things sometimes elude those who are strong independent thinkers. Ah, here's my book. (picks up a book lying on the table and turns the binding towards her to read the title)

DIRECTION: *The two dons exit right stage.*

LIGHTING: Fadeout with the exception of a spot on the OLDER SAYERS as she returns to her desk.

OLDER SAYERS: (resting her cheek in her hand) Would that Oxford had been my lover. "I that am twice thy child have known thee, worshiped thee, loved thee, cried / Thy name aloud to the silence and could not be satisfied . . . Bear with me as thou hast borne with all thy passionate throng / Of lovers, [and] the fools of love . . . ".[5]

End Scene 2

ACT I
Scene 3

LIGHTING: Fade in to reveal the YOUNGER SAYERS' London apartment (1923).

5   Dorothy L. Sayers, "Lay." Op. I (1916) Verse II.

MUSIC: Whispering (1920) – Paul Whiteman or similar dance song comes from a victrola/ phonograph.

DIRECTION: *The YOUNGER SAYERS' back is to the door. She is doing a Black Bottom step in the middle of the living room while holding a long cigarette holder in one hand and a glass of Guinness in the other. BILL WHITE enters left stage wearing a motorcycle outfit. He makes a sheik headdress using a sash and scarf. The YOUNGER SAYERS appears to be oblivious to his presence.*

BILL WHITE: (calls her name over the music as he comes through the door) Dorothy. Dorothy. (sneaks up from behind turns off the victrola and grasps her in a Rudolph Valentino-like fashion while carefully avoiding the cigarette and glass)

YOUNGER SAYERS: (mildly surprised, playfully) Are you sneaking up on me?

BILL WHITE: (still grasping her) Yes. And I have caught you by surprise.

YOUNGER SAYERS: (flippantly, Holmsian) Not true. I heard your motorcycle round the back.

BILL WHITE: (still holding her, he speaks romantically in French then in English) *Ma Chéri, laissez-moi vous montrer tout ce que le monde a de merveilleux.* My darling, let me show you the wonders of the world.

YOUNGER SAYERS: (playfully, romantically in French then English) *Ainsi, nous parcourrons les vastes océans.* We shall sail the oceans far and wide.

BILL WHITE: (releases her and falls into a chair with a work-worn sigh and removes the headdress) What shall we do tonight?

YOUNGER SAYERS: Bill . . . how about murder in an advertising agency?

BILL WHITE: I think you had better wait until they raise your salary.

YOUNGER SAYERS: My Lord Peter might just make a go of it. He could make his entrée at Benson's disguised as a junior copywriter and . . .

BILL WHITE: You haven't answered my question. Some of the gang want to go dancing at the Palais.[6]

YOUNGER SAYERS: I don't want to disappoint you Bill, but I've been a bit queer today.

BILL WHITE: You don't look ill to me. In fact, I think you're in rather good spirits this evening.

YOUNGER SAYERS: Just trying to distract myself. One mustn't give in to these things.

BILL WHITE: (encouragingly) Let's bike over to that fish and chips. You've always liked the food there.

YOUNGER SAYERS: Good idea. The thought of cooking just now doesn't appeal to me.

DIRECTION: *They exit left stage.*

6   Hammersmith Palais a popular London dance hall frequented by Dorothy L. Sayers and Bill White.

LIGHTING: Spot on OLDER SAYERS.

OLDER SAYERS: (with humor, nostalgia) I certainly had a
lot of energy in those days . . . racing around on the back of
Bill's bike . . . dancing the night away. (with resignation and
relief) On the other hand, being married to him would have
been a disaster. And he was beastly unhappy about being
father. But if I had done things differently, there'd be no John
Anthony.

End Scene 3

ACT I
Scene 4

LIGHTING: Fade in to reveal a doctor's office/surgery
             (1923).

DIRECTION: The DOCTOR is sitting at her desk.

DOCTOR: (reads chart and picks up intercom or just
calls to NURSE in next room.) Sister, would you please
tell Miss Sayers to DOCTOR (CONT'D): come in and
hold my calls until further notice. (uses intercom or calls
a second time.) Oh Sister . . .

NURSE: (O.S.) Yes Doctor.

DOCTOR: I will have my tea now.

NURSE: (O.S.) Yes Doctor.

DIRECTION: *The YOUNGER SAYERS enters left stage and approaches the desk.*

DOCTOR: (cordially) Please have a seat. I've arranged for tea.

YOUNGER SAYERS: Thank you.

DOCTOR: (concerned) Your test result was positive. You're pregnant.

NURSE: (on the intercom or in person) Doctor, shall I bring the tea?

DOCTOR: Yes Sister. Thank you. (to the YOUNGER SAYERS) Dorothy, you know I'm your friend as well as your doctor. So please, let us be honest with one another. (looking at the chart) You have a good position at Benson's, but do you have the means to raise a child?

DIRECTION: *The NURSE enters left stage and sets the tea tray on a side table near the desk. She pours tea for SAYERS and hands her the cup.*

YOUNGER SAYERS: (taking the cup from the NURSE) Thank you Sister.

DOCTOR: Thank you Sister. That will be all for now. I will pour my own tea.

NURSE: Very good doctor.

DIRECTION: *NURSE exits left stage.*

DOCTOR: (tactfully, as she rises from her desk and pours her tea) May I ask whether you had taken precautions[7] . . .

YOUNGER SAYERS: (nervously) Yes. (sets her tea cup on the desk) Although I've always been put off by that sort of thing.

DOCTOR: Have you considered an alternative?

YOUNGER SAYERS: An abortion? (with determination) No Alice, I'm taking responsibility for the child.

DOCTOR: Dorothy, I commend you on your attitude towards life. And because you are so well educated, I don't presume to tell you the way of the world. But you have a very great task ahead. Is there any chance of your getting married?

YOUNGER SAYERS: (puts her head down) I can't say.

DOCTOR: Will you inform your family?

YOUNGER SAYERS: (anxiously) Oh no. They're getting on and I don't want them to worry. I –

DOCTOR: (interrupting her) I see. Well Dorothy, you know your own mind. It must be your decision. Sister will add you to the book and give you an appointment for next month. Will that be alright?

7   See Barbara Reynolds, Dorothy L. Sayers: Her Life and Soul (New York: St. Martin's Press) 1993, 121-22; also Sayers' letter to her mother 14 February 1919 in Barbara Reynolds, The Letters of Dorothy L. Sayers 1899 to 1936: The Making of a Detective Novelist (New York: St. Martin's Press) 1996, 150-51.

YOUNGER SAYERS: Yes. That'll be fine. Thank you Alice. You're a good friend. I'm grateful for your support.

DOCTOR: (with compassion while shaking the YOUNGER SAYERS' hand) Good bye Dorothy.

END ACT I

ACT II
Scene 1

LIGHTING: Spot on OLDER SAYERS.

OLDER SAYERS: How ironic it is that we should hold steadfast to an unrequited love and then bring children into the world by another. (picks up a picture frame on her desk) Dear Cousin Ivy,[8] may God reward you. You were so good to my little John Anthony. What a mother you made!

DIRECTION: *While the OLDER SAYERS is speaking, WIMSEY emerges center stage from the darkness and approaches the OLDER SAYERS' desk. He sits on the right corner of the desk, facing the audience. She is unaware of his presence because he remains invisible to her.*

OLDER SAYERS (CONT'D): (still holding the picture) And he loved you too. (replaces picture and begins busily taking notes from a book)

WIMSEY: On the 3rd of January 1924, Miss Dorothy L. Sayers gave birth to a healthy son. For all his charm, Bill made no apologies for his attitude towards fatherhood. And so to assist the new mother with the daunting task of raising a child alone, enter (spreads arms and bows from the waist while remaining seated on the desk) Lord Peter Wimsey, amateur sleuth and gentleman extraordinaire. (pause)

WIMSEY (CONT'D): Of course I'd been around a while before John Anthony was born. Let me see, how did she put it? That I "might go some way towards providing bread and cheese".[9] (picks up the picture frame and examines the photo with his monocle) Many a crime needed solvin' to keep Ivy's little charge in nappies, and later at Balliol. But I get ahead of myself. Bill got the push; Cousin Ivy took charge of the baby; and Dorothy, still smarting from the wounds of a former love, consoled herself, as was her habit, with work.

DIRECTION: *WIMSEY retraces his steps center stage disappearing into the darkness.*

LIGHTING: Fade in to reveal the copy room of an advertising firm (1926).

DIRECTION: *The 1ˢᵗ FEMALE TYPIST is typing and the 2ⁿᵈ FEMALE TYPIST is standing at a file cabinet looking through files. The MALE COPYWRITER is sitting at a desk editing a piece of writing. They are discussing the YOUNGER SAYERS' relationship with Mac Fleming. The room is smoky and on the walls are Guinness posters by Gilroy and Coleman's Mustard advertisements.*

SOUND: Telephone rings.

1ˢᵗ FEMALE TYPIST: (stops typing and answers the phone) Benson's advertising. May I help you? He's not in just now. Yes, let me take your number. (writes down the number)

9   See Sayers' letter to her mother n.d. November 1921. Barbara Reynolds, The Letters of Dorothy L. Sayers 1899 to 1936: The Making of a Detective Novelist (New York: St. Martin's Press) 1996, 181

1st FEMALE TYPIST (CONT'D): You're welcome. Good-bye. (returns to her typing without looking up) Say, I heard some news the other day about Dorothy's new chappie.

2nd FEMALE TYPIST: (turning around to face the others with a file folder in her hand) Do tell.

1st FEMALE TYPIST: (continues to type without looking up) It seems that Major Mac Fleming is divorced from his first wife (stops typing and looks up) who is still living (pause) and he has children.

MALE COPYWRITER: (as he vigorously scratches out several lines of the writing he is editing) He's a pleasant enough fellow.

2nd FEMALE TYPIST: Yes, and popular with the ladies too I imagine.

MALE COPYWRITER: Where did she meet him?

1st FEMALE TYPIST: I don't know. But I think he's some sort of journalist.

MALE COPYWRITER: They're both writers then.

1st FEMALE TYPIST: They seem alright together. Dorothy's rather cheerful these days.

2nd FEMALE TYPIST: I wonder what her parents think. After all, her father is rector of Christchurch. I don't suppose her family would approve of her marrying a divorced man.

1st FEMALE TYPIST: (takes a drag from a cigarette, electric if available, resting in an ashtray next to the typewriter)

1st FEMALE TYPIST (CONT'D): I expect she gets lonely. Aside from her work as a writer, she's always struck me as a rather private person.

2nd FEMALE TYPIST: That's true. But things are different now. It's 1926 and not everyone bothers about marrying a divorced person these days. And she's not young anymore.

MALE COPYWRITER: And we're not getting any younger standing around gossiping. I'm taking this copy upstairs. I think I see her coming down the hall.

DIRECTION: MALE COPYWRITER takes his paper and exits right stage. The YOUNGER SAYERS then enters left.

YOUNGER SAYERS: (exuberantly, one hand in the pocket of her tailored jacket, holding a medium sized cigarette holder in the other with a file under her arm) Good morning everyone!

1st FEMALE TYPIST: Good morning. 2nd FEMALE: Good morning.

DIRECTION: The YOUNGER SAYERS hands the file to the 1st FEMALE TYPIST.

YOUNGER SAYERS: (a little rushed) Here's the Coleman file. You must excuse me. I have an appointment with my publisher.

1st FEMALE TYPIST: Of course.

2nd FEMALE TYPIST: (with sentiment) Lord Peter Wimsey . . . It must be wonderful to be a writer of detective stories.

YOUNGER SAYERS: Yes, it is gratifying . . . Although I have to admit that the demands of an aristocratic protagonist can be rather trying at times. Well, I mustn't be late. (turning to leave, then facing them again with humor) Lord Peter does insist on promptness when it comes to meeting with the publisher. Cheerio.

DIRECTION: The YOUNGER SAYERS exits left stage.

End Scene 1

ACT II
Scene 2

LIGHTING: Spot on OLDER SAYERS.

OLDER SAYERS: Poor old Mac. God rest his soul. He suffered much during those last years . . . the effects of the war, the gas, fits of temper . . . they sometimes made our life a misery.

LIGHTING: Fade in to reveal the YOUNGER SAYERS, now in her 40's, sitting at a desk in her study.

SOUND: Door slams off stage.

DIRECTION: *Her husband MAC who has been drinking, but holds his liquor well, enters left stage with a whiskey glass.*

MAC: (supporting himself on the back of a chair) Dorothy . . . Mrs. Fleming. Can I have a moment of your time?

YOUNGER SAYERS: (looking up from her work) Mac dear what is it?

MAC: I need some food.

YOUNGER SAYERS: (kindly) Alright dear. Go have a lie down and I'll bring a tray to your room.

MAC: (bordering on obnoxious) I don't want a lie down. Come here. I'll show you what I want.

YOUNGER SAYERS: (getting up from her desk) I'll ask Cook to fix you something. I won't be a moment.

DIRECTION: *The YOUNGER SAYERS exits right stage.*

MAC: (gropes his way around the chair and collapses in it, then repeats her words in a mocking tone) I won't be a moment.

DIRECTION: *MAC falls asleep while sitting up in the chair. His hand is still holding the whiskey glass which is resting on an end table.*

LIGHTING: Spot on OLDER SAYERS.

DIRECTION: *The OLDER SAYERS gets up from her desk and walks over to MAC sleeping in the chair. She carefully removes the glass from his hand, covers him with a small lap rug, and stands in front of him. He remains oblivious to her presence.*

OLDER SAYERS: Harriet Vane, how I envied you your Lord Peter . . . to be rescued, to be adored . . . These things I exchanged for another life. And I married Mac for better or for worse. I'd be lying if I said it was all bad. But being on one's own again after 24 years of marriage does have its benefits. Forgive me dear. (kisses him on the forehead) I know you did your best. But if I had done things differently . . .

LIGHTING: Fadeout except for spot on OLDER SAYERS as she returns to her desk and is seated.

DIRECTION: *WIMSEY emerges from the darkness center stage, walks over to the OLDER SAYERS, and sits on the right-hand corner of her desk facing the audience. He picks up one of her books, turns it in his hand and examines the title on the binding. He then adjusts his monocle, opens the book, scans a few pages, closes and replaces it.*

WIMSEY: Unlucky in love she may have been, and in that . . . (as if having a sudden revelation) or perhaps because of it, I too have suffered much romantic disappointment and seemingly endless frustration . . . But at least she was not unlucky when it came to tellin' a good detective story. And tell 'em she did . . . in novels and short stories . . . Maybe . . . (tapping his temple with his forefinger) if we concentrate, we can revive the muse. You remember how the audience brought back Tinker Bell in Peter Pan . . . And I still have a few good crimes left in me. Maybe we can encourage her to write just one more story. (slips off the desk) Shall we give it a go?

DIRECTION: WIMSEY *retraces his steps center stage disappearing into the darkness.*

END ACT II

ACT III
Scene 1

LIGHTING: Fade in to reveal the elegant but tasteful
             1930's apartment of LORD PETER WIMSEY.

MUSIC: Classical piano music.

DIRECTION: *WIMSEY is playing the piano dressed in a
             smoking jacket.*

BUNTER: (enters left stage) My lord, Miss Vane has just
rung up and asked me to give you a message.

WIMSEY: (crestfallen) Oh Bunter, she hasn't canceled our
dinner this evening?

BUNTER: No my lord, but she will be delayed due to "an
unforeseen circumstance".

WIMSEY: Bunter, are you deliberately trying to drive me
to distraction?

BUNTER: No my lord. I am repeating Miss Vane's words
not mine.

WIMSEY: (exasperated) Very well then man, out with it!
Did she <u>name</u> the cursed blighter, the stranger in black, the
unnatural hag, the tormentor who threatens to overshadow

WIMSEY (CONT'D): our long overdue assignation? (pause) And not to put too fine a point on it, there's your own predicament to be considered.

BUNTER: My predicament my lord?

WIMSEY: Your painstaking preparation of the meal!

BUNTER: I always anticipate the unexpected my lord and the meal, or my predicament as you put it, is already well in hand. But in answer to your first inquiry, yes, Miss Vane did apprise me of her particular circumstance.

WIMSEY: Confound you man. Must I extract the information through torture? (momentarily covering his face with his hands) I have neither the strength nor the inclination to match wits with you today.

BUNTER: Forgive me my lord if I made light of the occasion. I was insensitive to your anxiety that all go well. I should have realized you are not yourself. (pause) Miss Vane asked if it would be alright for me to collect her half an hour later than arranged. She explained that the "unforeseen circumstance" was a sudden insight regarding the plot for her new novel.

WIMSEY: (with relief) Ahhh!

BUNTER: She said that she would be most grateful if she could use the extra time to make a few notes.

WIMSEY: There is no need for you to apologize, Bunter. It is I who must once again beg your forgiveness. I am

WIMSEY (CONT'D): sure I don't know what came over me. Give her all the time she needs. Then go and fetch her. Take the Daimler.

BUNTER: Very good my lord.

DIRECTION: *BUNTER exits left stage. WIMSEY walks over to the fireplace and retrieves his pipe from the mantle. Standing in front of the fire, he begins to fill it with tobacco.*

LIGHTING: Spot on OLDER SAYERS.

DIRECTION: *The OLDER SAYERS is busily working on her new murder mystery. WIMSEY emerges from the darkness center stage wearing his smoking jacket, pipe in hand and approaches the OLDER SAYERS' desk. He stands on his tiptoes and makes an effort to peer at what she's writing.*

WIMSEY: (addresses the audience) We're off to a good start. A bit wordy in places . . . but I like it. Now . . . (puts his pipe in his mouth and slides his palms back and forth a few times) who's going to be the victim? Not even I know what's going to happen ahead of time. At present, I'm looking forward to my dinner with Miss Vane. Bunter must be on his way back by now. Let us return.

LIGHTING: Fade in to reveal WIMSEY'S apartment.

MUSIC: Classical piano music begins.

DIRECTION: *WIMSEY has changed into his dinner jacket and has resumed playing the piano. A spectacular fresh flower arrangement has been placed on top of the piano. BUNTER and HARRIET enter left stage. HARRIET is laughing, presumably at a remark or joke told by BUNTER. WIMSEY immediately rises from the piano and greets her.*

WIMSEY (CONT'D): At last, my Beatriiiceee[10] has arrived!

DIRECTION: BUNTER takes HARRIET'S coat. She is dressed in an evening dress. As she walks toward the center of the room, WIMSEY comes to meet her and gallantly kisses her hand.

HARRIET: Hello Peter. (teasingly) And so Dante and his Beatrice are reunited.

WIMSEY: (offering her a white flower from the arrangement on the piano) And tonight all the world . . . and this apartment has just become a Paradise.

DIRECTION: BUNTER approaches WIMSEY and HARRIET. He is carrying a tray with two glasses of sherry.

HARRIET: I'm flattered Peter . . . (picks up a glass of sherry) Thank you Bunter. (to WIMSEY) But I believe (cups her other hand near her mouth as if she is going to say something secret) we've been called upon to solve a mystery.

WIMSEY: (takes a glass from the tray, bows and clicks his heels) And so we shall.

DIRECTION: BUNTER carrying tray exits right stage.

10 Play on the name Beatrice.

WIMSEY (CONT'D): (offering his arm) Let us first investigate Bunter's *filet de sole* with sauce *mousseline sabayon.*

DIRECTION: *HARRIET graciously accepts WIMSEY'S arm and they exit right stage.*

LIGHTING: Fadeout except for spot on OLDER SAYERS.

DIRECTION: *The OLDER SAYERS rises from her chair and paces the area around her desk talking aloud to herself.*

OLDER SAYERS: I'm perplexed. I was sure my Lord Peter would remain comfortably retired. But I suddenly find myself compelled, by some force I know not what, to tell another story. Well, no matter. I've already set the scene. And now for the murder . . . How shall it be done? (thinking) No . . . No, first we must have a victim. Shall I assassinate a politician? Condemn a cardinal? A pair of lovers perhaps? No, let's keep it simple. I think our victim will be someone of average importance, modest income . . .

DIRECTION: *The OLDER SAYERS returns to her desk and continues to write in her copybook.*

OLDER SAYERS (CONT'D): Hummm . . . Now what doom shall befall said victim?

LIGHTING: Fade in on WIMSEY'S apartment while maintaining a spot on OLDER SAYERS.

DIRECTION: *WIMSEY and HARRIET have finished dinner. They enter right stage and sit across from one another in the living room. BUNTER then enters right stage with the coffee tray.*

BUNTER: (while serving the coffee) My lord, since you yourself will be driving Miss Vane home, I would like to step out for a while.

WIMSEY: Certainly Bunter. It's the least one can do for so superb a chef!

HARRIET: Your *soufflé glacé au citron* was *magnifique*!

BUNTER: Thank you my lord. Miss Vane. I am most gratified.

WIMSEY: Goodnight Bunter!

HARRIET: Goodnight Bunter!

DIRECTION: *BUNTER leaves the coffee tray so that WIMSEY and HARRIET may pour themselves a second cup and exits right stage.*

WIMSEY: Right. (setting his coffee cup on the table) Shall we nip across the way (nodding in the OLDER SAYERS' direction) and see how the muse has arranged things for us?

HARRIET: (putting down her coffee cup) Oh absolutely. Lead on Peter.

DIRECTION: *WIMSEY and HARRIET walk across the stage towards the OLDER SAYERS' desk.*

LIGHTING: Full stage on both WIMSEY'S apartment and on the OLDER SAYERS.

WIMSEY: (with reverence in a lowered tone) She is preoccupied with the sublime act of creation.

HARRIET: Yes. (leaning over the desk beside WIMSEY to watch the OLDER SAYERS work) I wonder how many novelists ever consider their position in terms of the sublime. Imagine if my detective hero, Robert Templeton,[11] began accepting bribes to conceal evidence, an alteration someone might easily make with the stroke of a pen. It would utterly demoralize my readers for whom Templeton has become an inspiration!

WIMSEY: I quite see what you mean. Come my Beatrice, let us return to my diggings and await her pleasure—the *modus operandi*.[12]

DIRECTION: *WIMSEY and HARRIET saunter back across the stage to WIMSEY'S apartment. WIMSEY walks over to the fireplace mantle, empties and refills his pipe. HARRIET sits in a chair near the fire and takes a cigarette from a box on the table. WIMSEY lights her cigarette. They are both facing in the direction of the OLDER SAYERS.*

OLDER SAYERS: Perhaps a shooting?

LIGHTING: Instant blackout leaving all the actors in the dark. The lights immediately return revealing a shadowy area center stage.

11   Harriet Vane's fictional detective hero.
12   Mode of operation.

DIRECTION: *Inside the shadow there are two individuals clothed in black, the* VICTIM *and the* MURDERER, *who stand facing one another. In response to the* OLDER SAYERS' *suggestion of a shooting, the* MURDERER, *on the left, steps back from the* VICTIM *pulls out a gun and shoots him.*

SOUND: Gunshot.

DIRECTION: *The* VICTIM *falls but both individuals remain within the shadowed area.*

OLDER SAYERS: A shooting is so common. (vigorously erases her writing) Maybe . . . a stabbing.

DIRECTION: *The* VICTIM *stands and both individuals face one another again. The scenario is repeated with the exception of the type of killing. In this instance, the* MURDERER *takes out a knife and stabs the* VICTIM.

SOUND: A grunt.

DIRECTION: *The* VICTIM *falls.*

OLDER SAYERS (CONT'D): Too bloody. (vigorously erases her writing) Perhaps a strangling.

DIRECTION: *This time* MURDERER *steps behind the* VICTIM *and strangles him.*

SOUND: Choking noise.

DIRECTION: *The* VICTIM *falls.*

LIGHTING: Spot on WIMSEY and HARRIET

HARRIET: I say Peter. (holding out her hand and examining her fingernails) I do wish she would make up her mind.

WIMSEY: (looking at his pocket watch) I think it's about time for . . .

HARRIET: The blunt instrument! WIMSEY: The blunt instrument!

DIRECTION: *This time the MURDERER holds an object high over his head and clobbers the VICTIM.*

SOUND: A thud.

DIRECTION: *The VICTIM falls. WIMSEY and HARRIET clap their hands in applause.*

OLDER SAYERS: (erasing vigorously) Too obvious. I've got it!

WIMSEY: She's got it!

HARRIET: She's got it! Oh, I do hope it's not a poisoning.

LIGHTING: Blackout.

SOUND: A frightful scuffle and a sharp agonized cry.

LIGHTING: Fade in to reveal only WIMSEY'S apartment and a spot on the OLDER SAYERS.

HARRIET: What do you make of that Holmes?

WIMSEY: I say, the game's afoot!

SOUND: Telephone rings.

WIMSEY (CONT'D): Excuse me Harriet.

DIRECTION: *WIMSEY exits right stage to answer the phone.*
              HARRIET goes over to the piano and admires
              the flower arrangement. She also examines a
              photograph or two and perhaps a painting on
              the wall. WIMSEY returns with a worried
              look.

HARRIET: Peter, what's wrong?

WIMSEY: That was Inspector Parker. Bunter is being detained on suspicion of murder.

End Scene 1

ACT III
Scene 2

LIGHTING: Fade in to reveal an interrogation room at
             the police station.

DIRECTION: *BUNTER is facing left stage; his back is to*
             WIMSEY who has just been escorted into the
             room by a POLICEMAN.

WIMSEY: Bunter, turn around and look at me.

BUNTER: I cannot my lord.

WIMSEY: Don't be an ass man. I don't believe for a minute that you've done anything despicable.

BUNTER: (turning around and facing WIMSEY) That isn't the point my lord. Your reputation . . . I –

WIMSEY: My reputation be damned! It's you I'm concerned about. How did you get into this filthy mess?

DIRECTION: INSPECTOR PARKER *enters right stage and joins WIMSEY in the room.*

PARKER: (to WIMSEY) They're still trying to recover a body.

WIMSEY: (to BUNTER) Sit down Bunter. You couldn't have been gone for more than an hour.

DIRECTION: BUNTER *sits on a chair.* WIMSEY *also sits but PARKER remains standing.*

PARKER: (to WIMSEY) Peter, I'm sure we can get this straightened out. But as I told you on the phone, there are three witnesses who testified seeing Bunter in an altercation with the victim who then collapsed. After that, your man was seen to drag the body into the back of his car and drive off. One of the witnesses said he had heard the man mention the Addison Hotel. They also gave us the number of Bunter's car.

WIMSEY: (to BUNTER) What say you Bunter?

BUNTER: Yesterday I received a phone call from a Mr. Alfred Kline. He said that he too was in service and that

BUNTER (CONT'D): I was highly recommended as someone who, being connected with the famous criminologist Lord Peter Wimsey, might be of assistance in the way of detecting things. It seems his employer turned him out of the house without explanation. Considering that he might be suspect of some wrongdoing, he asked if I would help him to investigate the matter. He then suggested that we meet at The King's Wood for a pint. And since I saw no harm in meeting at a public place I agreed to his proposal. When I arrived, there was a man standing . . . well just barely standing outside the pub and he appeared to be heavily intoxicated.

DIRECTION: POLICEMAN enters right stage hands PARKER a note and exits.

PARKER: (reads the note) Salcombe Hardy[13] has just descended upon us. I wonder how the press got hold of it so quickly.

WIMSEY: (suspiciously) Hmmm. (to PARKER) Steady old man. (pauses and rubs his chin while thinking) Sooo "that way goes the game"[14] . . . (to BUNTER) Go on Bunter.

BUNTER: Well my lord, as I approached the pub entrance, the intoxicated man began calling my name. I asked if he was Mr. Kline. He nodded and stumbled forward. I quickly reached out for his arm to steady him but he took a swing at me and hit his fist on a lamp post. He felt that alright and then began mumbling something about the Addison Hotel and collapsed. I thought I had better get him into the car since he could not return to the pub. Then without further difficulty, I drove to the hotel. The clerk confirmed

---

13   Fictional news reporter created by Dorothy L. Sayers.
14   Shakespeare, <u>A Midsummer Night's Dream</u> III.2.289.

BUNTER (CONT'D): that Mr. Kline had been staying there. After putting him to bed, I left a note explaining the circumstances and within minutes of leaving the hotel, I was intercepted by the police.

WIMSEY: Charles, have you checked Bunter's story?

PARKER: We have. The hotel clerk, who claims to have been on duty all evening, denies ever meeting an Alfred Kline or speaking with a Mr. Bunter. In fact, the description Mr. Bunter gave of the hotel clerk in no way matches the description of the man we questioned tonight. Bunter said the clerk had red hair and was clean shaven. My man said the clerk had black hair, a mustache, and wore wire-frame spectacles.

WIMSEY: Did you also speak with the hotel owner?

PARKER: He's on holiday and the clerk was working alone.

WIMSEY: Alone?

BUNTER: It's a very small hotel my lord. Not at all the sort of establishment a man of means would . . .

PARKER: Yes, yes. That would account for the lack of staff.

WIMSEY: Bunter, when you encountered Mr. Kline outside the pub was there anyone else around?

BUNTER: I couldn't say my lord. It was dark and I didn't expect to find Mr. Kline in that condition. It rendered me more or less senseless to my surroundings.

WIMSEY: Of course. (to PARKER) Charles, produce these lying blackguards who claim to be witnesses.

DIRECTION: *A POLICEMAN enters right stage, hands PARKER a bowler hat and a shoe, and then remains standing in the room.*

PARKER: (to the POLICEMAN) Where were these found?

POLICEMAN: We found them shoved in a hedge near the hotel Inspector.

PARKER: Is this the hat and shoe Mr. Kline was wearing tonight?

BUNTER: Yes, I believe those are his.

WIMSEY: What is the name of Mr. Kline's employer?

BUNTER: I did not discuss the particulars with him on the phone my lord.

WIMSEY: Well since you undressed him and put him to bed, you might be able to provide us with a clear description of his appearance.

BUNTER: Unfortunately, he became combative again once we arrived at the hotel. The clerk unlocked Mr. Kline's room and helped me to lay him on the bed. Luckily, his room was on the ground floor and since he would not allow us to undress him, I just covered him with a blanket. I did notice, however, that he seemed a young man, not at all like someone who had been in service for very long.

WIMSEY: Alright Bunter, while Charles and I investigate this situation you had better go and rest.

DIRECTION: *The POLICEMAN escorts BUNTER from the room.*

End Scene 2

ACT III
Scene 3

LIGHTING: Fade in to reveal WIMSEY'S apartment.

DIRECTION: *HARRIET is sitting on the sofa facing WIMSEY who is standing at his place by the mantle. They each have a whiskey and soda.*

WIMSEY: It was so good of you to wait for me.

HARRIET: I couldn't desert Bunter . . . and . . . (looking up at WIMSEY, her hesitation indicating that she meant to say, "and you")

WIMSEY: (from the heart) Harriet . . .

HARRIET: (stands to divert WIMSEY'S attention from her) Now that you have told me Bunter's side of the story, what about these witnesses?

WIMSEY: (offers HARRIET a cigarette from a box on the table and takes one himself, lights HARRIET's, then his own) Yes, the three students who claimed to be standing within sight of The King's Wood.

DIRECTION: HARRIET *resumes her place on the sofa.*

WIMSEY (CONT'D): Inspector Parker, my beloved brother-in-law,[15] is willing, for the moment, to overlook their insinuation that murder has been done . . . reason being that their testimony so closely matches Bunter's. However, we still have the hotel manager to reckon with and the mysterious absence of Mr. Kline.

HARRIET: Did the police inspect his room at the hotel?

WIMSEY: Empty. Although there was evidence to suggest that someone had occupied the room recently.

HARRIET: And the hotel book?

WIMSEY: The previous occupant was a Mr. W. H. Smithington.

HARRIET: And I suppose there was no one available who could give a description of Mr. Smithington.

WIMSEY: Correct my dear Watson.[16] What we need is a clue. Come Doctor.

DIRECTION: WIMSEY *sets his drink on the mantle and extends his hand to assist HARRIET from the sofa. They walk towards the OLDER SAYERS left stage.*

---

15   Married to Wimsey's younger sister, Lady Mary Wimsey.
16   Friend and assistant to Sherlock Holmes.

LIGHTING: Spot on OLDER SAYERS working at her
            desk.

DIRECTION: *HARRIET and WIMSEY wander around the
            OLDER SAYERS' desk trying to get a peek at
            what she is writing. WIMSEY stands behind her
            and looks over her shoulder. HARRIET begins
            carefully shuffling through a few papers on the desk.*

HARRIET: Can you see anything?

WIMSEY: No. How about you?

HARRIET: Here's something . . . (disappointed) Oh, it's
only a shopping list. Wait a minute . . . there's something
written in the margin. (turns the paper horizontal and reads
aloud) The Red-Headed League.

WIMSEY: Harriet, let us commit our clue *possiblé* to memory and return to Baker Street.

LIGHTING: Slow fadeout on OLDER SAYERS.

DIRECTION: *WIMSEY and HARRIET begin walking
            across the stage to WIMSEY'S living room.*

HARRIET: I have every confidence in you Holmes.

WIMSEY: Shall we then announce the bans and name the
day? We have just spent our first night together.

HARRIET: Peter, what time is it?

WIMSEY: (looking at his pocket watch) It's 5:00 in the
morning.

DIRECTION: *They arrive at the living room.*

WIMSEY (CONT'D): And with the dawn so rises my suspicion regarding this case. Make a note Harriet.

SOUND: Telephone rings

WIMSEY (CONT'D): Excuse me.

DIRECTION: *WIMSEY exits right stage. HARRIET retrieves a pad and pencil from the table and sits on the sofa. WIMSEY returns and paces the floor.*

WIMSEY (CONT'D): That was Charles. He's coming round. Now where was I? We have three witnesses identified as students, a hotel clerk, and if you will excuse the expression, the missing carcase of Mr. Kline.

HARRIET: What about The Red-Headed League?

WIMSEY: Yes – (interrupted)

DIRECTION: *PARKER enters left stage.*

PARKER: Good morning. (with gentlemanly acknowledgement) Harriet.

HARRIET (smiling) Chief Inspector.

WIMSEY: Charles, you're just in time. Have a seat.

DIRECTION: *PARKER takes a seat and WIMSEY walks over to the fireplace and fills his pipe.*

WIMSEY (CONT'D): I think we're entitled to a writ of habeas corpus. That hat and single shoe sticking out of a hedge . . .

PARKER: I have to admit Peter, it has greatly added to the confusion.

WIMSEY: What was the age of the hotel clerk?

PARKER: He was a young man . . .

WIMSEY: And the hotel? Have you found out anything more about the Addison?

PARKER: (hesitatingly as if anticipating something unexpected) Yesss . . . as a matter of fact, it's rather popular with students during the hols.

WIMSEY: No doubt. Now I think we might risk a tiny celebration. (to PARKER, offering him a cigar from a humidor on the table) Have a cigar.

PARKER: Thank you. (lights the cigar) Now what exactly are we celebrating?

WIMSEY: Why Bunter's exoneration!

PARKER: Actually Peter, we've turned up another piece of evidence.

WIMSEY: (looking up) Why O gods must you forever take your pleasure in beguiling the children of men?

PARKER: We have a set of finger prints from Mr. Kline's room which proves Bunter was there last night.

WIMSEY: Of course he was there! In spite of a marked talent, not unlike my own, for the occasional deception, my man is not a liar! In fact, I can remember when he made a very convincin' news reporter . . .

PARKER: Please be serious Peter. You know I would release Bunter in an instant if it were up to me. But we must examine the evidence.

WIMSEY: Those finger prints can only mean the hotel clerk is lying.

PARKER: I'm not disputing that, but what reason would a hotel clerk have to lie about a kindly citizen escorting an inebriated guest to his room?

HARRIET: Remember there were two different clerks.

PARKER: That's right. And the one we questioned said he had been on duty all evening. It seems we may have two lying clerks.

HARRIET: Yes. And therein lies another mystery. What happened to the clean-shaven red-haired clerk described by Bunter?

WIMSEY: What indeed? Did you make a thorough search of the hotel?

PARKER: From top to bottom.

HARRIET: What about the three witnesses?

WIMSEY: Have you detained them for further questioning?

PARKER: No. We took their names and addresses. And since they were inebriated we sent them home to sleep it off.

WIMSEY: Charles, I think you'll find they had reason to give you false information.

HARRIET: You mean that one of them could have been a murderer?

PARKER: Peter, when I arrived you intimated by way of suggesting a celebration that the case was solved. What was the meaning of that?

WIMSEY: With the application of a little logic, this case practically solves itself.

PARKER: I'm listening. I admit I'm somewhat surprised, considering Bunter's dilemma, at your increasingly flippant attitude.

WIMSEY: Never let it be said that for one moment, I ever made light of my man's misery. How could I when it's my other self you have locked away and . . .

PARKER: You're not on trial Peter. You said something about the application of logic . . .

WIMSEY: Let us ask ourselves, Why Bunter? Out of all His Majesty's loyal subjects to choose from, they singled out the one man in England least likely to commit such a crime.

PARKER: That, Peter, goes without saying . . .

HARRIET: You're implying then that this was no random occurrence.

WIMSEY: Given the hypothesis that life itself is fraught with seemingly random occurrences, logic dictates no other course.

PARKER: Could there be something from Bunter's past, some vendetta perhaps?

WIMSEY: Alas, poor Bunter . . . nothing to raise the hairs on one's head. No, I don't believe it is anything so dramatic as a scandalous past.

PARKER: I believe you are having us on. You already know the answer, so why the long explanation?

HARRIET: I'm afraid that Peter and the gods have something in common: they both take mischievous pleasure dabbling in the affairs of men. And at poor Bunter's expense . . . Really Peter.

WIMSEY: Harriet, you wound me. Without further delay, I shall continue. I began with the premise that Bunter is innocent of any wrongdoing. Next, I went over the details of his story and the testimony of the alleged witnesses. Why didn't they lend Bunter assistance in his effort to restrain the obnoxious Mr. Kline? Why stand on the sidelines?

HARRIET: Of course. If they were close enough to hear what was being said, it's only logical that they could have lent some assistance.

PARKER: I see that. Strange that they did nothing even though Mr. Kline threw a punch at Mr. Bunter.

HARRIET: You were interested, Peter, in the age of the hotel clerk . . .

WIMSEY: Did you find it strange that Bunter should have described Mr. Kline as someone rather young to be in service to a gentleman?

PARKER: That observation did not escape me, but how do you link it to Mr. Kline's disappearance?

HARRIET: What about our clue . . .

WIMSEY: Patience dear heart . . .

PARKER: You've discovered a clue?

WIMSEY: More of a key I think, although I don't know if it will be of much interest to you . . .

PARKER: Let me be the judge of that.

HARRIET: It was the title of a mystery: The Red-Headed League.

PARKER: And I suppose Mr. Sherlock Holmes, or should I say Arthur Conan Doyle holds the answer to Mr. Kline's whereabouts?

WIMSEY: In a manner of speaking, I suspect so.

HARRIET: (to WIMSEY) I too am wondering how this clue, or key as you put it, ties in with our mystery.

PARKER: How did you manage to come up with a clue when you've been at home all evening?

WIMSEY: Yes, well aside from that, I believe you already hold enough plain evidence, without said clue, to solve this mystery.

PARKER: I've never been more ready for an explanation.

WIMSEY: Would you first like to hazard a guess?

PARKER: I suppose you're going to tell me there never was a Mr. Kline.

WIMSEY: Now you're getting warm.

HARRIET: And the two hotel clerks and the student witnesses are somehow linked together.

PARKER: On any other day, I might want to pursue this line of reasoning with you. But Mary has been waiting for me since last night. It's now breakfast time . . .

WIMSEY: The crime, my friends, was one of deception, a ruse. Picture if you will three students with more time on their hands than brains or finer feeling. The hols have just begun, and in a show of bravado one of them suggests a daring caper . . . the outsmarting of Lord Peter Wimsey. They may have gotten the idea from a newspaper article or some other source . . . maybe even from one of your books Miss Vane. I'm sure Parker will . . . how do the Americans put it, teach them to sing like canaries . . . But my guess is that after several pints they believed themselves invincible.

PARKER: I think I'll make some arrests, but not until I've had my breakfast. And I'll contact Sally with a fair warning about the thing going to press.

WIMSEY: I'd appreciate that. I believe you'll find your three culprits holding out at the Addison. You might try looking for a bloke with a bandaged fist.

HARRIET: Our Mr. Kline.

WIMSEY: Just so.

HARRIET: You mean this whole affair has been nothing more than a sinister plot intended to deceive you and Mr. Bunter.

WIMSEY: A very dangerous plot . . . made all the more so by their failure to recognize that deceiving the police would lead to their own downfall.

HARRIET: (thoughtfully) So one of them posed as the intoxicated Mr. Kline. That would explain Bunter's observation of his youthful appearance. The other as the hotel clerk . . . probably employed there during the hols. Oh wait a minute, there were two clerks.

PARKER: That's right. And they could have switched places before my man arrived. (pause) On the other hand, Bunter's clerk might have altered his appearance.

HARRIET: And then one of the three must have notified the police and given the number of Bunter's car.

PARKER: Yes, and put the hat and shoe into the shrubbery to further the impression of foul play. But we still have a

PARKER (CONT'D): problem . . . How could all three of them have been at The King's Wood posing as inebriated witnesses and be at the hotel carrying out their scheme at the same time?

WIMSEY: Patience Alexander, your Gordian Knot[17] is about to be undone.

HARRIET: That's not too difficult.

WIMSEY: (to PARKER) There you see, the Oracle,[18] she speaks.

HARRIET: The question we must ask is whether we want to accept as evidence the students' claim that they were ever at The King's Wood. Is there anyone who can corroborate their story?

PARKER: The proprietor at The King's Wood said he could not recall serving anyone who fit their description.

WIMSEY: They could have imbibed anywhere before arriving at The King's Wood. But Harriet's right. It's only logical to assume that they wanted us to believe they had been outside The King's Wood all along, when in reality they were playing their parts elsewhere.

PARKER: So by the time my men intercepted Bunter leaving the hotel, they had cast off their various disguises . . . except for the clerk . . . and were heading for The King's Wood.

HARRIET: Yes. And they believed that by becoming inebriated, or at least acting as if they were, and claiming they

17 Associated with the legendary exploits of Alexander the Great and popularly used as a metaphor to describe a complex problem.
18 Source of wise counsel or prophetic speech.

HARRIET (CONT'D): had been standing around The King's Wood all evening, they could effectively cover their tracks. But Peter, all of this still doesn't explain –

WIMSEY: Our single clue . . . The Red-Headed League, that famous case where Holmes exposes a couple of opportunists who invent a false organization and then disguise themselves to carry out their sinister plot. Thus I was able to deduce that since the paper on which the title of the famous case was written lay in plain sight, and therefore recently penned, the current affair involving Bunter may have found its inspiration in the former. And then there was Bunter's mention of the red-haired individual, a trifle perhaps to some, but to me a fiery spark that set all my suspicions ablaze.

HARRIET: Brilliant!

PARKER: I wonder who alerted Salcombe Hardy.

WIMSEY: There's no accountin' for where Sally gets his information. But I suspect this night's escapade was intended as a cruel prank masterminded to catch yours truly and his ever-wary sleuth's assistant and faithful man off their guard.

PARKER: Peter, would you and Harriet like to accompany me to the station for Bunter's release?

WIMSEY: By all means.

End Scene 3

ACT III
Scene 4

LIGHTING: Fade in to reveal the police interrogation room.

DIRECTION: *WIMSEY, PARKER, and HARRIET enter right stage.*

PARKER: (to WIMSEY) I'm glad we were able to resolve the case amicably and that you and Bunter decided not to press charges.

HARRIET: Strange that they should have returned to the hotel.

WIMSEY: Yes. But that's only because they were so intent on incriminating Bunter they didn't anticipate being arrested themselves.

PARKER: As soon as they realized we had the Addison surrounded they came quietly.

WIMSEY: And there was no need to subject Bunter to making an identification because as soon as I revealed to them how we uncovered each detail of their plot, and produced the disguises found in their rooms, they were ready to confess.

HARRIET: I suppose the last thing they expected was to come face to face with Lord Peter Wimsey when they arrived at Scotland Yard.

PARKER: After being photographed and fingerprinted and shown to one of the Yard's best rooms reserved especially for young men of their ilk, they decided that a life of crime should not be an easy one and swore never to deceive the police or anyone else again. Had they not been students, it would have gone much harder with them. (to WIMSEY) By the way Peter, where did you find that clue you mentioned earlier?

WIMSEY: Charles old man, let that be a mystery we shall endeavor to resolve another day.

DIRECTION: The POLICEMAN and BUNTER enter left
              stage. After escorting BUNTER into the room
              the POLICEMAN exits.

WIMSEY (CONT'D): (to BUNTER) Ah Bunter, free at last. I hope those blackguards, those minions of dissipated youth who have so sorely misused you appreciate your dropping the charges. Is it not one of the follies of the young, the mark of grossest ignorance to act without ne'er a thought to the consequence?

BUNTER: I think my lord, I should like to go home now.

WIMSEY: Harriet, let us escort our man home and tuck him into bed.

HARRIET: (linking her arm to BUNTER'S and smiling) Yes. "The prisoner is discharged without a stain upon [his] character."[19]

END ACT III

19 Dorothy L. Sayers, Triple Wimsey: Three Lord Peter Wimsey
    Mysteries, Strong Poison (New York: Harper & Row) 1985, 251.

INTERMISSION

ACT IV
Scene 1

LIGHTING: Spot on OLDER SAYERS.

DIRECTION: *WIMSEY emerges from the darkness center stage.*
He is wearing his academic robe and a wreath of
laurel leaves on his head. Draped over one arm is
another academic robe and Somerville cap.

WIMSEY: G. K. Chesterton, a figure much admired by
Sayers, explains that (delivers quote in Chestertonian
style) "the aim of a mystery story, as of every other story
and every other mystery, is not darkness but light. [. . .]
The climax must not be only the bursting of a bubble
but rather the breaking of a dawn [. . .] The secret may
appear complex, but it must be simple; and in this also
it is a symbol of higher mysteries."[20] (pause) In 1944,
ever in search of the clue that would provide a deeper
understanding of life's mystery, Dorothy L. Sayers began
a passionate, thoroughly satisfying affair with Italian
poet Dante Alighieri. The relationship resulted in a
three volume translation of The Divine Comedy, an allegory of the soul's journey in the afterlife. It is our wish
to pay homage to the work of this Literary Great and

20 G. K. Chesterton, "How to Write a Detective Story" (1925).

WIMSEY (CONT'D): his esteemed translator. (lowering his voice slightly, moving towards the OLDER SAYERS with stealth) As I approach, she will recognize me only as that other Poet who long ago accompanied Dante. And yet unlike the 13th Century original, we will journey to a different realm. Inspired by Sayers' 1947 essay "The Lost Tools of Learning," we will enter (raising his voice and his forefinger with affected pomp) The Divine Akademeia.

DIRECTION: *WIMSEY holds forth the robe. The OLDER SAYERS stands and he helps her to put it on. He offers her the cap and she puts it on herself.*

OLDER SAYERS: I think I should know you. Are you not Virgil?

WIMSEY: It suffices to say that I am your guide.

OLDER SAYERS: Then lead on my laurel-wreathed tutor.

DIRECTION: *They slowly walk towards center stage.*

LIGHTING: Fade in to reveal an ancient Athenian ruin illuminated by the colors of the sunset (as opposed to a Dantean wood). There are Greek pillars standing or lying here and there. There is also a torch (or special lighting effect to suggest a torch flame) burning on an altar in the background.

DIRECTION: *Sitting on a marble step playing a harp is the legendary Greek hero Akademos. He is wearing a short toga and sandals.*

AKADEMOS: (stops playing his harp) Welcome, welcome to the Academy. I see that you are friends of academe and so have arrived most opportunely. I am Akademos, the appointed caretaker of this place. Regrettably, it no longer functions as the center of philosophical inquiry established by our father Plato, but serves only as the silent acropolis beyond which lay two roads, (pointing right stage) the one, the way of Ignorance, the other, (pointing to the torch flame and speaking with passion) Enlightenment! (returns to playing his harp in low soothing tones)

WIMSEY: What say we take this road to perdition, and with a little good fortune at our side, return once more to what that great man Lewis has described as "the sunlit lands"[21] above.

OLDER SAYERS: I see a sort of gate, (pointing towards the right stage exit) there, in the distance.

WIMSEY: Yes. (pointing) And there is writing at the top . . .

DIRECTION: The gate is off stage.

AKADEMOS: (stops playing his harp and recites, from memory, the passage over the gate) It reads: "YOU WHO HAVE PUT ASIDE THE TOOLS OF LEARNING ENTER BY ME. YOU WHO HAVE ABANDONED BELIEF ENTER BY ME. YOU WHO HAVE ABAN-DONED REASON ENTER BY ME AND BEHOLD THE RADIANT FACE OF SOPHIA NO MORE."

LIGHTING: Fadeout on AKADEMOS.

21 C. S. Lewis, The Silver Chair (New York: Harper Trophy) 2000, 140.

DIRECTION: WIMSEY and the OLDER SAYERS move towards the right stage exit.

WIMSEY: (looking upward at the writing and speaking to the gate as they exit right stage) Shall we then, who are merely curious enter by ye and hope, from the lesson learned, to do the world a better turn?

DIRECTION: WIMSEY and the OLDER SAYERS exit right stage.

End Scene 1

ACT IV
Scene 2

LIGHTING: Fade in to reveal a political rally and THE POLITICIAN standing behind a podium.

DIRECTION: WIMSEY and the OLDER SAYERS enter left stage.

OLDER SAYERS: Whew! How hot it is inside this gate.

THE POLITICIAN: My friends gather round. You're just in time for my oration.

DIRECTION: As THE POLITICIAN gives his speech, he is engulfed in flames (created by special lighting effects) that rise and grow brighter after every

sentence. Gathered around him are a few onlook-
ers who clap and hurrah.

THE POLITICIAN: Under my leadership there will be freedom
of choice for everyone. Freedom is about choosing your own way
of life. You must stand by your opinions. And, as your leader, I
will fight to uphold your right to choose silencing the voice of
the opposition. Your destiny is your own and together we will
shape your future. Together we can discover a path for you.

WIMSEY: (speaking over THE POLITICIAN'S voice to
the OLDER SAYERS) Methinks he's a politician.

OLDER SAYERS: (interrupting THE POLITICIAN) I say,
are you not burned by the flames?

THE POLITICIAN: (loudly) Burn? There are no flames here,
only words . . . words to change the course of history, words
to bring down kingdoms and give birth to new civilizations,
words to bring a mindless rabble, by its own choosing, under
submission. And let history record (raising his forefinger and
pointing in the direction of the onlookers) that by words alone
one can conquer an empire, and so influence a nation there
will no longer be any need for religion, for morals or tradi-
tion. Words are no respecter of persons. And with the power
of words, one can so change the face of a civilization, (pretends
to crush something in his fist) like crushing an egg before it is
hatched, its progeny will simply cease to exist . . . (opens his
fist and pretends to blow something off his palm, speaking in
a quieter tone) and be no more. (the flames about him now
seem to suddenly burn white hot)

DIRECTION: *The POLITICIAN'S AUDIENCE reaches out*
and gives congratulatory handshakes and hur-
rahs to THE POLITICIAN.

WIMSEY: (an aside to the OLDER SAYERS) I'd gladly withstand the lettered ranting of a Machiavelli[22] o'er the ravings of this hypocritical windbag any day.

OLDER SAYERS: "How laudable it is for a prince to keep good faith and live with integrity . . ."[23]

DIRECTION: *WIMSEY and the OLDER SAYERS move right stage.*

WIMSEY: Let us move on. This place grows cold despite its flames.

DIRECTION: *WIMSEY and the OLDER SAYERS exit right stage.*

End Scene 2

---

22   Niccolò Machiavelli (1469-1527) popularly associated with political ruthlessness and cunning.
23   Niccolò Machiavelli, The Prince and the Discourses (New York: The Modern Library) 1950, 63.

ACT IV
Scene 3

WIMSEY: (O.S.) I see a spacious quad before us.

OLDER SAYERS: (O.S.) An Oxford college?

LIGHTING: Fade in to reveal a college quad of a non-descript institution.

DIRECTION: *WIMSEY and the OLDER SAYERS enter left stage. Numerous holes in the ground are indicated by dark patches and shadows on the stage floor.*

WIMSEY: It's hard to say. There are so many holes in the ground . . . (steering her away from a large hole) Mind your step.

DIRECTION: *THE SCHOLAR, dressed like a don in academic robe, enters left stage, rushes past WIMSEY and the OLDER SAYERS and mounts a raised speaker's platform center stage. He holds a book in his hand.*

WIMSEY: Perhaps this don will speak with us. (to THE SCHOLAR) Excuse me sir . . .

THE SCHOLAR: (standing on the speaker's platform) Children, you hold your future in the palm of your hand. The

THE SCHOLAR (CONT'D): very future of education, indeed of the human race, depends on the choices we make today . . . What sort of animal is a Trivium? Something with three legs? And what about that timeworn quartette we call the Quadrivium. I grant you, these are the cords that have bound, no, have enslaved us to the past. But they have outlasted their usefulness and are no longer to be relied upon as the sole means of acquiring an authentic education. There is no room here for such *laudator temporis acti*.[24] We are on the brink of understanding everything! If only the theologians and the do-gooders would step out of the way.

DIRECTION: *After every few remarks there is an explosion and a flash of light somewhere on the ground. THE SCHOLAR is surrounded by onlookers clothed in academic attire who clap after every explosion.*

OLDER SAYERS: (to THE SCHOLAR) What is causing these explosions? Is the university at war?

THE SCHOLAR: Explosions? War? These eruptions are but the flashes of great insight! We who are the learned, the educators, the scientists, we are the makers and shapers of the future. We are the craftsmen of a better world. In our milieu no one is bound to the slavery of right and wrong, (tilts his hand back and forth with disdain) this and that.

DIRECTION: *As THE SCHOLAR concludes his/her harangue, the explosions and flashes of light gradually come closer to WIMSEY and THE OLDER SAYERS.*

---

24   Praiser of times past, from "The Lost Tools of Learning" (1947) given at Oxford by Dorothy L. Sayers.

THE SCHOLAR (CONT'D): (slaps his palm on the book) Here we scrutinize all things and are free of moral platitudes,

SOUND: Loud explosion.

THE SCHOLAR (CONT'D): religious restrictions,

SOUND: Louder explosion.

THE SCHOLAR (CONT'D): and blessedly, of those abominable, cursed and unproven absolutes!

SOUND: Loudest explosion.

DIRECTION: *The final explosion and flash of light comes so close to WIMSEY and the OLDER SAYERS that they must jump out of the way to avoid being hit.*

WIMSEY: (to the OLDER SAYERS as they move away from THE SCHOLAR) I can remember a few professors like that. I wonder if this learned don was tutor to our politician.

OLDER SAYERS: I smell a lovely fragrance. Why it's oil paints and linseed. Perhaps we have come to the end of this place and will begin to see some improvement here.

WIMSEY: We have indeed reached the end but must descend a little lower now before we can return.

DIRECTION: *WIMSEY and the OLDER SAYERS exit right stage.*

End Scene 3

ACT IV
Scene 4

LIGHTING: Fade in to reveal THE ARTIST standing at
his easel painting a picture. Around him is
devastation and chaos.

DIRECTION: *WIMSEY and the OLDER SAYERS enter
left stage stepping over garbage strewn on the
floor.*

SOUND: Pitiful wailing and moaning of men, women
and children.

OLDER SAYERS: (covering her ears) Such wailing and tra-
vail! I can hardly bear it.

THE ARTIST: Wailing? I hear only those melodies created
by the most talented musician – one who expresses reality.
He has captured the moment and has given it back again
full of life, pathos, and creative possibility.

WIMSEY: Such a sound unnerves my soul. This cacophony
of human suffering you call music?

SOUND: Wailing and moaning slowly fades.

THE ARTIST: What after all is music? What is any art?
My painting for instance . . .

OLDER SAYERS: (leaning forward to scrutinize the painting) It is rather dark . . . Do you not feel . . . well, isn't it rather dehumanizing to express oneself in quite that way?

THE ARTIST: Dark? Yes. I express what is.

WIMSEY: And what do you contribute by your art?

THE ARTIST: You sound like a moralist. Art is not bound by morals, responsibilities and obligations. It must be free. It must be an expression of my relationship with everything around me. My contribution as you put it, although I hardly see what art has to do with paying a debt to humanity, is my perspective.

OLDER SAYERS: You feel no responsibility then?

THE ARTIST: To whom? We are artists! Suppose you were a film director. Would you allow the audience to dictate to you your proper job? Of course not! If the work offends, depresses, stimulates a libido or two what is that to you? Artists are not responsible for their works' reception. (fanatically) A work of art is alive, (bowing to WIMSEY and the OLDER SAYERS) and we artists are merely its humble creator!

DIRECTION: *WIMSEY and the OLDER SAYERS begin to walk towards the right stage exit.*

OLDER SAYERS: I've always believed in doing one's proper job, in using one's time and talent to creatively express ideas and opinions. But I can see how these craftsmen, though they do not deserve the title, have clearly traded the truth for a lie, and so by the works of their hands have damned themselves.

WIMSEY: Sentenced to remain forever adrift on an ocean of ignorance.

OLDER SAYERS: I pity the beholder of such works . . . the unwary victims of corruption doomed to spread their evil fruit.

WIMSEY: These are indeed sad lessons, and not to be easily dismissed. But the time has come now to take that other road, (raising his hand to indicate above) "The . . . hemisphere [that] doth o'er thee lie . . ."[25]

DIRECTION: *WIMSEY and the OLDER SAYERS exit right stage.*

End Scene 4

---

25 Dante Alighieri, <u>The Divine Comedy: Hell</u>, Trans. Dorothy L. Sayers (London: Penguin Books) 1949, Canto XXXIV, Ln. 112.

ACT IV
Scene 5

LIGHTING: Fade in to reveal a scene similar to Plato's allegory of the cave.

DIRECTION: *WIMSEY and the OLDER SAYERS now reverse the order of entry, entering right stage instead of left. They discover THE STUDENT and THE TEACHER bound to either side of a column. In front of each a silent shadow-puppet show is being performed.*

LIGHTING: Spot on THE STUDENT.

OLDER SAYERS: (addressing THE STUDENT) Why are you lashed to that pole? What crime could such a young student be guilty of?

THE STUDENT: It is not the lash that binds me. I was given wrong information and as a result made poor choices. It is the consequence of my choices that bind me so.

WIMSEY: And this silent performance . . . what purpose does it serve?

THE STUDENT: It is the reenactment of all my choices whether due to misinformation or the lack thereof. I am forced to relive each of these moments fully aware now of my error in judgment.

OLDER SAYERS: If you were given falsified or insufficient information why must you endure this isolation, this deafening silence?

THE STUDENT: I allowed myself to be seduced by those in authority who told me things that were pleasant to hear. Weep not for me. My days here are mercifully numbered. But know then that choosing according to one's fancy, to accept things at face value, whether through misappropriated trust, admiration or laziness, without taking the time to investigate the facts can only lead to the most abominable sort of loneliness. To be separated from the truth, cut off from reason, the consequence of a poor choice made against one's conscience is finally the cruelest of punishments.

LIGHTING: THE STUDENT is shrouded in darkness.

DIRECTION: *WIMSEY and the OLDER SAYERS walk around the pillar to speak with THE TEACHER.*

WIMSEY: Pray *magistre*, what is your story?

THE TEACHER: I am restrained by failing in my mission as a teacher. My fate is to repeatedly witness the suffering caused by giving poor instruction. Although I desired the best for my students, I secretly feared being at odds with the college, losing my livelihood and the respect of my peers. I have been given to understand how I have betrayed history itself through certain omissions and distortions, thus failing its lessons and perpetuating its errors. I have betrayed the trust of those under my tutelage. And I have traded the hard won freedoms, for which so many have shed their blood, for simple convenience. In this state I must remain until justice for my crimes has been satisfied.

WIMSEY: (to THE TEACHER) You tell a sad tale *magistre*, but alas one that is all too common.

LIGHTING: THE TEACHER is shrouded in darkness. There is a brief fadeout and immediately light begins to emanate from the right stage entrance.

DIRECTION: *The center stage is cleared except for WIMSEY and the OLDER SAYERS.*

OLDER SAYERS: (pointing right stage) Look! Someone approaches.

DIRECTION: *BOETHIUS enters right stage. He is in the company of seven women beautifully costumed in medieval attire[26] signifying THE SEVEN LIBERAL ARTS. Three signifying the Trivium are grouped on one side of BOETHIUS and the Quadrivium on the other.*

LIGHTING: Each of the seven women are illuminated by a different gemstone color: Ruby for Grammatica, Yellow Topaz (citrine) for Dialectia, Sapphire for Rhetorica, Emerald for Arithmetica, Aquamarine for Astronomia, Amethyst for Geometria, and a rainbow of pastel color as refracted from a diamond for Musica.

BOETHIUS: From time to time I walk these halls to console and to release from bondage those ready to embrace that sweet Lady, Wisdom.

OLDER SAYERS: Who are you?

26   For suggestions see Philosophy Presenting Boethius with the Seven Liberal Arts (1460-1470) by French painter Coëtivy Master.

BOETHIUS: My name is Boethius. And I too was once a prisoner, though not of error. I, as I am sure you two learned companions already know, was enamored of Poetica dictated by the honey-tongued muse and remained so until Philosophia opened my eyes and set my feet upon a wiser path. Follow me then and these seven handmaids ever at my side. I shall introduce them to you, each one. And by the time you've met them all, we shall have arrived at that blessed realm where all have been taught "how to learn for themselves"[27] and where, after having defeated the enemies of Wisdom, they may forever enjoy the wine of enlightenment!

DIRECTION: As each of THE SEVEN LIBERAL ARTS is introduced, the women come forward one at a time and move center stage. Each woman is holding a symbol of her art: Grammatica carries a book, Dialectica carries a miniature Greek pillar, Rhetorica carries a miniature podium, Arithmetica carries an abacus, Astronomia carries a telescope, Geometria carries a compass, and Musica carries a harp. Graciously, with a small bow, each holds out her symbol so that the audience can identify it. After each has been introduced they retake their places at BOETHIUS' side.

BOETHIUS (CONT'D): (steps forward) Behold: the Trivium, the first of which is Lady Grammatica. Clarity of speech is her art, for a Word well spoken once set the whole of the universe in vibrant motion. Lady Dialectica, who some call Logic, is the child of witty wisdom and the cornerstone of Faith. Lady Rhetorica, words she does not waste but her speech like a well aimed arrow ne'er fails to hit the mark. And now I give you the Quadrivium: Lady Arithmetica, she, like her sister Musica, confers the joy and the promise

27   "The Lost Tools of Learning."

BOETHIUS (CONT'D): of infinite possibility. Lady Astronomia who, beginning with the Star of David, draws us ever upward towards salvific wholeness to that "Jerusalem above".[28] Lady Geometria, kin to the very spheres, reminds us of our destiny, and beautiful Lady Musica whose song transforms and binds the rest in grace-filled harmony. Be not deceived by their feminine guise for like "the axe and the wedge, the hammer and the saw, the chisel and the plane . . ." they are fit for the battle and "adaptable to all tasks."[29]

WIMSEY: (moves a little down stage and delivers an aside to the audience) I say, if Lady Rhetorica doesn't resemble my Miss Vane . . .

OLDER SAYERS: (to BOETHIUS) What grace and bearing I see before me.

BOETHIUS: (to the OLDER SAYERS) Take my arm good lady. And as we walk, we shall discourse further on the qualities of these doughty maids.

DIRECTION: The OLDER SAYERS takes his arm.

WIMSEY: (to BOETHIUS) Lead on good teacher. (offers his arm to LADY RHETORICA who is HARRIET VANE in costume) In such good company we can do ought but follow.

DIRECTION: All exit left stage.

End Scene 5

28 Galatians 4:26.
29 "The Lost Tools of Learning."

ACT IV
Scene 6

LIGHTING: Fade in to reveal a backdrop of pastel cur-
tains hung in regal fashion gently swaying
to give the impression of a light breeze
blowing through the windows of a palace hall. (A fan may be used to simulate
this effect.) A couple of Greek columns are
suitably placed at either end of the palace
room.

*DIRECTION: BOETHIUS still arm in arm with the
OLDER SAYERS and WIMSEY arm in
arm with LADY RHETORICA enter right
stage.*

BOETHIUS: I have enjoyed our conversation immensely
and here I must leave you. For I have much work to do in
that other place.

OLDER SAYERS: Will I remember this fond dream?

BOETHIUS: Alas my good lady who can say? But now you
are ready I think for something rather stronger . . . "Go
now, ye strong, where the exalted way / Of great example
leads. Why hang you back? / Why turn away? Once earth
has been surpassed / It gives the stars. "[30]

30 Boethius, <u>The Consolation of Philosophy</u> (London: Penguin
Books) 1969, 146

DIRECTION: *Boethius bows and kisses the OLDER SAYERS'*
hand, steps back and waits for LADY RHE-
TORICA to take her leave from WIMSEY.

WIMSEY: (to LADY RHETORICA) Adieu my Lady, in
most beauteous guise, (bows and kisses her hand) my Miss
Va –

LADY RHETORICA: (holding her finger mischievously
to her lips and bending slightly forward toward WIMSEY)
Shhhh!

DIRECTION: *BOETHIUS offers his arm to LADY RHE-*
TORICA. She accepts it and they exit right
stage. Immediately afterward a joyful chant
begins and bright lights sway and dance over
the heads of WIMSEY and the OLDER
SAYERS. The CHILDREN of LADY WIS-
DOM, individuals of different nationalities
dressed in joyful colors representing various
periods in history, enter right stage and gather
in two or three small friendly groups. Some
are holding goblets of wine. They are engaged
in heady conversations, sometimes laughing,
sometimes patting one another on the back and
expressively using their arms and hands to
communicate.

LIGHTING: Dancing beams descend lower and engulf
WIMSEY and the OLDER SAYERS.

OLDER SAYERS: (looking up) What bright faces I see!
Who are these contented babes that laugh and make merry
overhead?

> *DIRECTION: LADY WISDOM enters left stage wearing a golden robe and jeweled crown.*

LADY WISDOM: I am Lady Wisdom, whom the Greeks call Sophia. These are my children, (indicating the various groups on stage) all favored to dwell in this mansion with me. (indicating over their heads) But these above hold a special place. From birth they were schooled on their parents' knee and by them given the tools of learning, some at great sacrifice. But be not distressed by their juvenile countenance. It is only an outward expression of their preserved innocence and childlike joy. For it has been given to just such as these to grow in wisdom and stature to the benefit of many.

OLDER SAYERS: I hardly deserve to be here and to behold such a heavenly vision.

LADY WISDOM: Ah my daughter, you misrepresent yourself. My house is not difficult to find. The way begins with every choice. And those who find me choose not for themselves but for the good of all. For I may also be found wherever there is compassion and justice, truth, and beauty. For the greatest of Wisdom's gifts is the respect for life and for the dignity of each human being. (cheerfully with emphasis) And now there is but one last vision you are favored to behold, someone here with whom I wish you to be reunited.

> *DIRECTION: ADÈLE[31] enters left stage in a blaze of light.*
> *She is dressed in white with a circlet of gold*

---

31 Befriended by Dorothy L. Sayers while working in France. See Sayers' letter to her mother 23 November 1919. The Letters of Dorothy L. Sayers 1899-1936: The Making of a Detective Novelist. Ed. Barbara Reynolds (New York: St. Martin's Press) 1996, 159-60.

*around her head. In her hand she holds a
long stem red rose. She bows to LADY WIS-
DOM who presents her to the OLDER
SAYERS. LADY WISDOM exits left
stage.*

ADÈLE: I am Adèle whose child you saved when you
became my good benefactor, Heaven sent, and taught
me that abortion is a sin. For that life "the Primal Good
inspires,"[32] and for my happiness, (kisses the OLDER
SAYERS on the cheek and hands her the red rose) accept
this token of my gratitude.

DIRECTION: *The OLDER SAYERS reaches out for the rose
and holds it by the lower stem. Both women
remain facing one another, ADÈLE still holding the upper stem. Both are reluctant to part
from one another.*

SOUND: An Oxford University bell rings.

WIMSEY: There is a familiar sound . . . (listens) engaged I
have no doubt to call us back from our reverie.

DIRECTION: *ADÈLE walks backwards a few paces retrac-
ing her steps, smiles, then turns and exits left
stage.*

END ACT IV

---

32 Dante Alighieri, The Divine Comedy: Paradise, Trans. Dorothy
L. Sayers and Barbara Reynolds (London: Penguin Books) 1962,
Canto VII, Ln. 142.

ACT V
Scene 1

LIGHTING: Spot on WIMSEY and the OLDER SAYERS.

DIRECTION: *Having completed their journey, WIMSEY and the OLDER SAYERS return from The Divine Akademeia and emerge from the darkness center stage. They are no longer in academic costume. WIMSEY escorts the OLDER SAYERS to her desk and pulls back her chair so she may sit. She is still holding the rose given to her by ADÈLE and her attention is so absorbed by it that she is no longer aware of WIMSEY. She raises the rose to her nose, smiles at its fragrance, places it in a vase on the desk and is seated.*

WIMSEY: (to the audience) She is once again unaware of me as that Peter of good repute. Therefore, we shall continue with our Sayersian hymn. "Through midnight waters mighty Tom will call."[33] And sailing into the mists of an enchanted dawn find ourselves once more in the City of Dreaming Spires.

LIGHTING: Fadeout left stage on the OLDER SAYERS and WIMSEY while simultaneously fading in center stage to reveal a college dinning hall.

---

33 Dorothy L. Sayers, "Lay." Op. I (1916) Verse IV.

DIRECTION: *Seated at the table are EMILY PENROSE, ALICE BRUCE, MILDRED POPE, the YOUNGER SAYERS, and two other SOMERVILLE DONS. On the table there are a few plates left over from the meal, a decanter, and wine glasses. WIMSEY enters right stage and introduces the scene. While he is speaking, the two SOMERVILLE DONS rise, silently excuse themselves, shake hands with the YOUNGER SAYERS and exit left stage. A SCOUT enters right stage, clears a few remaining dishes and exits.*

LIGHTING: Spot on **WIMSEY** as he moves center stage to introduce the scene.

WIMSEY (CONT'D): The year is 1920, mid October. Somerville is celebrating its long-awaited membership in the University. At age twenty-seven, Miss Sayers has returned to Oxford's hallowed halls to be awarded her BA and MA degrees. Let us now imagine that during her brief visit she has been asked to dine at the Fellows' table and there receive an irrefutable challenge to prove her mettle as a newly degreed woman of letters.

DIRECTION: *WIMSEY exits right stage.*

EMILY PENROSE: (to the **YOUNGER SAYERS**) It seems we four have been left to fend for ourselves? It was so good of you Miss Sayers to accept the Fellows' invitation to dinner. I hope you enjoyed the meal.

YOUNGER SAYERS: I'm having a splendid time. Thank you Warden.

MISS POPE: (to the YOUNGER SAYERS) I want to congratulate you again on the completion of your Tristan.[34] It's a fine translation.

YOUNGER SAYERS: Thank you Miss Pope. But you must also accept credit for its success.

EMILY PENROSE: What great lesson have you learned from the wide world since leaving us Miss Sayers?

YOUNGER SAYERS: Well apart from the struggle of having to shift for oneself . . . I mean, one is so well cared for here . . .

MISS POPE: Yes, we dons sometimes tend to be solicitous . . . although youth seldom appreciates the effort. Don't you agree Miss Bruce?

MISS BRUCE: Unfortunately, it's often looked upon as an intrusion rather than an asset.

YOUNGER SAYERS: A laxity in judgment for which I too must beg your pardons. But in answer to your question Warden, I've learned that an education is like sowing seed, and that in order for it to take root, the soil must first be tilled.

EMILY PENROSE: You're speaking of parents?

YOUNGER SAYERS: Yes. I think they should prepare their children to be educated, but not by heaping fact upon fact. They need to instill in them a love of learning.

34 Tristan in Brittany (1929). Poem translated by Dorothy L. Sayers from medieval French. It was not published in its entirety until ten years after its completion.

MISS BRUCE: Ah yes, a beautiful sentiment.

MISS POPE: That's as maybe. But beautiful sentiments rather go against modern theories of education.

EMILY PENROSE: The pragmatic approach. What can one teach a child whose head is already so full of such useful information?

YOUNGER SAYERS: "O brave new world that has such people in't![35]" . . . I often find myself shunning the madding crowd[36] of the "merely well informed"[37] and longing to be in the company of even the most humbly educated.

DIRECTION: *The four women laugh.*

MISS POPE: (refilling the YOUNGER SAYERS' glass from a decanter) I think Miss Sayers you are referring to character?

EMILY PENROSE: The acquisition of knowledge for its own sake can hardly be considered an education. A mistake frequently made by over anxious parents, sad to say.

MISS POPE: And unenlightened teachers.

YOUNGER SAYERS: I find one spends an unconscionable amount of time sifting through extraneous information in order to mine a few gems as it were.

---

35   The Tempest V.1.185.

36   Thomas Gray, "Elegy Written in a Country Churchyard" (1751)

37   From "The Aims of Education" (1916). A presidential address given by Alfred North Whitehead to the Mathematical Association of England. "A merely well-informed man is the most useless bore on God's earth."

EMILY PENROSE: This tilled soil you spoke of, shall we call it character?

MISS BRUCE: It does sometimes happen that a difficult student can be redeemed.

MISS POPE: Oh without question.

YOUNGER SAYERS: If one is up to the challenge.

EMILY PENROSE: (to the YOUNGER SAYERS) I gather you are speaking from experience? You taught high school if I remember.

YOUNGER SAYERS: Yes. At Hull[38] for four terms. Only I formed my opinion on the subject quite some time ago. My experience since leaving Oxford has served mainly to confirm that opinion.

MISS POPE: Do you believe boys and girls learn differently?

YOUNGER SAYERS: Should any of us be here if that were the case? But that doesn't answer your question. As individuals we all learn differently. And since sex is a difference, the answer is obvious.

EMILY PENROSE: That's a logical answer but not a very scientific one.

MISS BRUCE: Science has been used to justify a host of illogical premises. If given a choice, I personally prefer to err on the side of logic.

38 Girls High School in Hull, England.

EMILY PENROSE: I must concur. However, you will find that many people today will use science rather than logic to justify their positions.

MISS POPE: You are speaking again of the <u>merely well informed</u>.

EMILY PENROSE: Though the term lacks originality, it's certainly apropos for the modern attitude towards learning. A valuable lesson Miss Sayers.

YOUNGER SAYERS: It was a simple matter of deduction. I weighed the empirical evidence at hand and postulated the appropriate description.

MISS BRUCE: Now there's a fine example of a logical application of science.

MISS POPE: A field largely dominated by males.

MISS BRUCE: Yes, the very same field responsible for our modern theories of education.

EMILY PENROSE: I think I can see where this is going. Queensbery rules ladies.

MISS BRUCE: Of course Warden. We shall endeavor to make this an honorable argument. Although people tend to look upon a university education as a mark of prestige, I prefer to see it as a risk.

MISS POPE: Do you mean that although men and women may be equally educated they do not have the same opportunities?

MISS BRUCE: There is that aspect to consider. But the risk I'm speaking of has to do with the discovery that one's views are flawed or that one's feelings have been selfish. And then one must make a decision.

YOUNGER SAYERS: Since leaving Oxford, I have often thought about our place here. Oxford is centuries old and it seems like only yesterday women were allowed to tread the same footpaths as Wolsey and Donne.[39]

EMILY PENROSE: We owe a great debt to our predecessors. They fought a courageous battle to secure for women the right to higher education.

MISS POPE: You are among the first Miss Sayers to enjoy the spoils of victory. By wits alone we have fought the war against male opposition to our becoming members of the University.

EMILY PENROSE: By wits . . . yes Miss Pope, but I think not alone. I believe it had much to do with cooperation. And I think credit is due to every student who has come through these doors. And if I might add, we can never establish an equal relationship with those whom we think of as oppressors. We must learn from the past rather than dwell on its mistakes. The future of women's education now lies solely in the hands of the women themselves.

YOUNGER SAYERS: Yes! That's how I see it. I don't believe for a minute it was a man's choice to allow us to come here. It was Oxford itself that opened the doors. Women were ready to meet the challenge and Oxford responded in kind.

---

39 Cardinal Wolsey (c.1471-1530) and John Donne (1572-1631).

DIRECTION: *The three dons exclaim "<u>Hear, Hear</u>!". All four*
women then stand, raise and clink their glasses
together in a spontaneous salute: "<u>To Oxford</u>!".

End Scene 1

ACT V
Scene 2

LIGHTING: As the lights begin to fadeout on the din-
ing hall scene, WIMSEY in spotlight enters
right stage.

WIMSEY: Novelist, poet, playwright, Christian apologist,
Dorothy L. Sayers was all these things and more. Unim-
pressed with the pomp and circumstance that accompanies
worldly achievements, she preferred to concentrate on the
spiritual and intellectual fruits of her labor. For Sayers,
words carried no weight unless heeded, and action no merit
if not for the good of another. She put little faith in a scientific method that did not liberate and preserve the dignity
of the individual. Towards the end of her life she wrote and
spoke passionately about the things that really mattered.
And for Dorothy, what mattered most was life!

LIGHTING: Spot on OLDER SAYERS.

DIRECTION: *She is sitting at her desk writing a letter.*

OLDER SAYERS: (reading aloud to herself as she writes)
Dear Madam, Thank you for your interest. I shall do my

OLDER SAYERS (CONT'D): best to address your concerns. But be warned, I am no theologian. Commonsense and logic have always been my stock in trade. And yet, we should never depend wholly on our own judgment as the sole criteria for ethical decision making. But I trust you need not be told this. However, a proper reminder of our finitude never does one any harm. . . . You have asked me, "What advice can I give to the future?". I believe you will find the answer in my book, The Mind of the Maker. Please refer to the line, "Whosoever will be a lord of life, let him be its servant."[40] Are we not rapidly moving into an era where everyone fancies himself an independent?

DIRECTION: *She rises from the chair and paces as she speaks, the palms of her hands resting on the backs of her hips.*

OLDER SAYERS (CONT'D): Is the water independent of the kettle that holds it? Separate yes, but independent? Is the child independent of the womb? The answer should be obvious to even the most unscientific. In like manner, one can no more be independent of the society in which one lives than properly identify oneself using a *nom de plume*.[41] Or, as a point of contention in my own case, neglect to use my full Christian name. . . .[42] Let those who fancy themselves educated put their scholars' minds to the task. If we are to understand our place in the universe, even to remain civilized . . . we must put aside such notions of independence. We must raise ourselves up . . . not only to become the servants of life (with calm gravity) but its defenders! . . . Lastly, you speak of Oxford . . . My opinion on the subject is

40 Dorothy Sayers, The Mind of the Maker (New York: HarperCollins) 1989, 186.
41 Pen name.
42 Sayers insisted that her middle initial be retained whenever her name was used. See Barbara Reynolds, Dorothy L. Sayers: Her Life and Soul (New York: St. Martin's Press) 1993, 361.

OLDER SAYERS (CONT'D): this: you must not regret your not having been to Oxford. Of all the things I learned there, the most important was a respect for intellectual integrity. Now one does not need to cross an ocean to discover that bit of wisdom, invaluable as it is. Such a gem is not the sole property of an Oxford college . . . But perhaps you would do well to think of Oxford not so much as a place, but as a habit of mind—an ethereal crucible, if you will, in whose fires the intellect may be shaped and melded.

LIGHTING: Fadeout on OLDER SAYERS as she returns to her desk and continues writing.

OLDER SAYERS (CONT'D): Well my friend, even Dante had to return from the Empyrean[43] . . . and so must we. I am enclosing with this letter a copy of <u>The Mind of the Maker</u>. . . . Yours most gratefully, DLS.

END ACT V

---

43   The highest Heaven where God and the Angels dwell.

EPILOGUE

LIGHTING: WIMSEY emerges from the darkness center
            stage. As he comes downstage, lights come
            up to reveal the same Oxford college back-
            drop that opened the play.

DIRECTION: *He is again dressed in academic robe with sub-
            fusc and monocle. Behind him are the OXFORD
            STUDENTS dressed in period clothing, some
            wearing college scarves and black academic
            gowns, mingling with one another.*

WIMSEY: (addressing the audience) What can be said of
Oxford may also be said of Dorothy Leigh Sayers. The magic,
the mystery, the arrogance, simple erudition, genius and pro-
fundity, the enigma that is both person and place, a woman
invigorated by the challenge of living and working in a man's
world, a woman who, while struggling with the responsibilities of unwed motherhood, was driven by the need to express
the whole of her humanity. C. S. Lewis put it rather well when
he said of Sayers' ability to use words, "She is first and fore-
most the craftsman, the professional".[44] (pause) In all of her
life and long career, Sayers never strayed far from Oxford. It
was always there for her, its influence observed in her novels and plays and in those inspired works that have come
afterward. Thanks to the mind of this maker, I will go on and

---

44 C. S. Lewis, Of This and Other Worlds (London: Fount) 1982,
    105.

WIMSEY (CONT'D): so will Oxford having been made richer for her presence. A woman of mystery with "a careless rage for life"[45] who, at the end of her days, was laid to rest in the Church of St. Anne[46] scarcely more than an hour from this ancient and enigmatic city. Ah, Oxford!

LIGHTING: Slow fadeout.

MUSIC: Allow for a few seconds of applause from the audience before instrumental music begins (e.g. Sweet Georgia Brown or Charleston – Savoy Orpheans or medley of songs).

LIGHTING: Full stage again with the exception of the OLDER SAYERS sitting at her desk.

DIRECTION: *WIMSEY is still standing center stage. The OXFORD STUDENTS behind him partner off and dance with one another. The dance steps are lively and full of energy with leg kicking. WIM-SEY motions right, then left stage, and the principle characters make their entrances from alternate sides. At the same time, the OXFORD STU-DENTS who have been dancing behind WIM-SEY exit alternatively. The principle characters partner off and dance. WIMSEY dances with HARRIET. EMILY PENROSE dances with MAC. JIM and TONY dance. MISS POPE dances with PARKER and MISS BRUCE*

---

45   A frequently quoted phrase used by Sayers to describe her turn of mind. See Barbara Reynolds, <u>The Letters of Dorothy L. Sayers 1899 to 1936: The Making of a Detective Novelist</u> (New York: St. Martin's Press) 1996, 227.

46   Located in Soho, London

dances with BILL WHITE. BUNTER cuts in to take WIMSEY'S place with HARRIET.

LIGHTING: Spot on OLDER SAYERS at her desk.

DIRECTION: *WIMSEY walks over to the OLDER SAYERS and extends his hand to assist her, then offers his arm to escort her center stage. Aware now of WIMSEY, she accompanies him center stage where they dance. The OLDER SAYERS dances as if she is remembering all the old steps of her youth. The other actors stop dancing and gather to watch WIMSEY and the OLDER SAYERS.*

MUSIC: Fades.

DIRECTION: *WIMSEY bows to the OLDER SAYERS then both WIMSEY and the OLDER SAYERS move backwards and join hands with the other actors. They all come forward and bow.*

LIGHTING: Fadeout and return.

DIRECTION: *The OLDER SAYERS and WIMSEY have moved down stage center and bow. The other actors continue to hold hands behind them. They move back again and join hands with the other actors. Immediately, the YOUNGER SAY-ERS enters right stage, moves center, and bows.* The other actors then come downstage and join hands with the YOUNGER SAYERS. They all bow for the last time.

LIGHTING: Fadeout.

THE END

AUTHOR'S NOTE:

The following appendix is included in response to a suggestion to modify the curtain call. In this way, the author hopes to retain the original integrity of the play while allowing for its adaptation to different venues. The author's permission is given to make use of this appendix in place of the play's original curtain call where appropriate.

APPENDIX

(shortened curtain call)

MUSIC: Allow for a few seconds of applause from the audience before instrumental music begins (e.g. Sweet Georgia Brown or Charleston – Savoy Orpheans or medley of songs).

LIGHTING: Full stage again with the exception of the OLDER SAYERS sitting at her desk.

DIRECTION: *WIMSEY is still standing center stage. The OXFORD STUDENTS behind him partner off and dance with one another. The dance steps are lively and full of energy with leg kicking. WIMSEY motions right, then left stage, and the principle characters make their entrances from alternate sides. At the same time, the OXFORD STUDENTS who have been dancing behind WIMSEY exit alternatively. The principle characters partner off and dance. WIMSEY dances with HARRIET. EMILY PENROSE dances with MAC. JIM and TONY dance. MISS POPE dances with PARKER and MISS BRUCE dances with BILL WHITE. BUNTER cuts in to take WIMSEY'S place with HARRIET.*

LIGHTING: Spot on OLDER SAYERS at her desk.

DIRECTION: WIMSEY *walks over to the* OLDER SAYERS *and extends his hand to assist her, then offers his arm to escort her center stage. Aware now of* WIMSEY, *she accompanies him center stage where they dance. The* OLDER SAYERS *dances as if she is remembering all the old steps of her youth. The other actors stop dancing and gather to watch* WIMSEY *and the* OLDER SAYERS.

MUSIC: Fades.

DIRECTION: WIMSEY *bows to the* OLDER SAYERS, *then the two bow to the audience. They move back and join hands with the other actors. Immediately, the* YOUNGER SAYERS *enters right stage, moves center and bows. The other actors then come downstage and join hands with the* YOUNGER SAYERS. *They all bow for the last time.*

LIGHTING: Fadeout.

THE END

ABOUT THE AUTHOR

VICTORIA NELSON is a freelance writer from California who holds an MA in English Literature from Holy Names University. She is a writing tutor for graduate students and a homeschool curriculum consultant. Other publications include a screenplay, <u>Jack Marlin, Private Eye: The Case of the Barbary Blackbird,</u> and a novel, <u>Romana Volume I</u> From the Annals of Romana. She is also a contributing author to the <u>Saint Austin Review</u> (<u>StAR</u>).

www.ingramcontent.com/pod-product-compliance
Lightning Source LLC
Chambersburg PA
CBHW031520040426

42445CB00009B/314